The Juice

The Juice

COLEMAN BARKS

HARPER & ROW, PUBLISHERS
New York, Evanston,
San Francisco, London

for Kittsu

Grateful acknowledgment is made to the following magazines in which
some of the poems first appeared: *Wisconsin Review, South Florida
Poetry Journal, Tennessee Poetry Journal, Lillabulero, Folio, ARX, Gnosis,
The Fiddlehead, Poem, Abraxas, Ann Arbor Review, New Generation,
Red Clay Reader, Wascana Review, Foxfire, Latitudes, Southern Poetry
Review, the goodly co, Kumquat, Hiram Poetry Review.*
"Adam's Apple," "Forehead," and "Tic" originally appeared in *Poetry
Brief,* edited by William Cole, published by The Macmillan Company,
© 1971 by William Cole.
"Choosing," "Nickajack Cave," "The Finger of Necessity," "Feather River
Valley, 1956," "The Truckdriver," "The Oracle," "Stomach," "Elbow,"
"Heart," "Brain," "Appendix," "Navel," "Ear Lobe," "Forehead," "Skull,"
"Scar," "Inner Ear," and "Bags Under the Eyes" originally appeared in
Quickly Aging Here, edited by Geoffrey Hewitt, © 1969 by Doubleday
and Company, Inc.
"Taste Buds" and "Spit 'n Image" originally appeared in *Earth, Air, Fire
& Water,* edited by Frances Monson McCullough, published by Coward,
McCann & Geoghegan, Inc. in 1971.

First Edition

Standard Book Number: 06-010213-6

Library of Congress Catalog Card Number: 70-156506

Contents

v

II. Choosing

III. *The Swim*

I. Body Poems

Big Toe

running running
running   but clean
as a referee's whistle

& absolutely still
within my shoe
inside my sock:

he listens for mud

Stomach

lunch paper sinking
into

the lake surface
the lake bottom

sleeping frogs
snapping turtles

Elbow

cradling my funnybone
like a child
I didn't mean to hit:

the dull ache, the surprise
at kissing myself
there

Cheek

somebody's hiding
in the drapes
I bet I know who:

No   it's just his shoes

Heart

an earthen
sound:

60 seconds later
the two all-clear
whistle notes

Brain

a flashlight
looking through the empty
limbs

Appendix

one boxing glove
laced up
and ready

Knuckles

under the bench
four helmets
look out backwards
at the cheerleaders:

each to his own

Navel

hold the phone
down here   see
if she can still
hear me gurgling:

my Long Distance
mother

Shoulder Blades

the common scallop
shell   broken in two
at its hinge

moves mystically
like it wasn't
hurt

Back Just Below the Shoulder Blades

the most kissed
stone tablet
at a sacred grotto:

the one nearest
where it happened

Jaw

the first balcony:

a secret conversation
with yourself:

eating popcorn
with your ears covered

Upper Lip

the pronouns
keep changing
from *myself*
to *yourself*
and back:

during a long kiss

Adam's Apple

never said
a word:

he just nodded

Small of the Back

water shapes you
as you lean back
up against the opening
filling the pool

Crown of the Hair

with the heel
of your hand
make a round place
in the sand

Tongue

this mealy earth,

my driveway

Arch of the Foot

going up in full gear
it's rung by rung
but coming down

the naked fireman
will often use the outside
of his ladder's legs

Downy Hair in the Shape of a Flame Moving up the Stomach and Ending at the Solar Plexus

anything this
recognizable

should have
a name:

Hair on the Toes

tiddledypom
doesn't keep on growing
tiddledypom
in fact it will
never have to be cut
hence the name:

pompoms
de la tiddlies

White Crescents at the Bottoms of Fingernails and Toenails

the edge of
a coat-of-arms:

who do you think you are

Bags Under the Eyes

the turnaround place
at the end of a lovers' lane:

why is that car coming back

Nape

there are names
for almost everywhere
loving,

Jowl

good-natured names
like land
that's been lived on:

Cowlick, Hollow of the Back

Ear Lobe

Suck Creek, Lovers' Leap
(we all know
 what happens there)

Kneecap

Island, where I live,

is one of thousands
you can visit

round like a
(a sporting good)

a hat of gristle
with my feelings

Cartilage

the mind crouches
over its fried chicken

then lifts off
my shinbone

Thighs

hoist & lever
in the water

constantly adjusting
their bite

Achilles Tendon

walk on your heels
across a puddle:

you mythological
beast

Wrist

minnows
are the little muscles
just under the surface

Hips

pumpkin
with pumpkin
hair & pumpkin
seeds inside

Eye

delayed light:

the flying
edge, and the wing
folded

Warts & Moles

are highway signs:

Next Exit ½ mi.
Food—Roomettes

Stuckey's
Interesting Gifts — Souvenirs

that's the same hitchhiker
we saw last night

Blood

the winery is on fire:

listen to the music

Semen

thousands
of weird little figurines
carved out of soap

suddenly come alive
and jabber like
foreigners

Forehead

the two main lines
of your palm fit
exactly over the ones
at the top of the
bridge of your nose:

what have you forgotten

Cavities

the scraps of old
addresses we carry
in our wallets

Roof of the Mouth

run your tongue
all along the rafters:

moth in a Coke bottle

Middle Finger

a country boy

with one joke
always:

hey, Zeke, where y'at

Genitals

the loaded question

the slick answer

Skull

a folk remedy
for the lovesick:

share a meal
of turtle meat

then tack the shell up
for a birdhouse

Spine

a curl of rainwater
down the windshield

moves around
like it's hearing
the radio

Coccyx

fear is a rattling
in the tailbone:

my saliva
thickens

Blind Spot

what no one can see
is always a point
widening in the eye

Lymph

, in thy origins
be all my sins
remembered

Scar

the one chance
I will ever have
to go to Finland

is a long lake
frozen to my leg

Pelvis

a great stainless
steel mixing bowl

(with me in it) floats
down the snowpath

Lap

says I'll wait for you
here

Skeleton

on this jungle gym

Buttocks

oceanic pods

drifting laterally

midway down

softly thinking

(for centuries)

sunlight   sunlight

Inner Ear

the girl on the dime

gets off one night
and meets me there

Goosepimples

crowdpleasers
coming down the aisles
of my arms and legs:

crowds of the pleased
stand up and clap

Shoulders

an afghan
covers my sleeping

back the way I look
at rolling
country

Liver

a dripping locker room
full of older men

Bruises

paint samples

Ankles

dice

(dance, you rascals)

Hair on the Chest

cash on the barrelhead

(who'll cover my bet)

Ring Finger

legend of
the hoop snake
same as

Palm

your lifeline's
partially true

Haunches

waterwitching bones
that hunker down

on the spur of the moment
like a spell

Calves

canvas swimming
pool floats rise

and sink in a deep
breathing exercise

Back of the Knee

a daily memo pad

open to the scratch
paper at the year's end

Dimple

a saltlick
for deer

Crook of the Arm

a half nelson

on the lamb

Top of the Head

clockwork:
the sprinkler's arc

comes round again
with its beer

Pupil

getting used to the dark
resting in touch and taste:

talking through the time
I take to change

This Poem Reflecting
in the Eye

your body
has some backwards
english
on it

Sleep

(formed in the edges)

touch the splinter

touch the white

Space Between the Two Front Teeth

do a ratface
at your dentist
's

Sole

solus, a, um
goes away back

to the first three
vertical steps

Spleen

in man a dark purplish flattened oblong
object of a soft fragile consistency ly-
ing near the cardiac end of the stomach
enclosed in an elastic capsule from which
bundles of fibres ramify through the tis-
sue of the organ which is divisible into
a loose red pulp in intimate connection
with the blood supply and a denser white
pulp chiefly of lymphoid tissue condensed
in masses about the small arteries: the
seat of emotions: the source of laughter

Fingertips

up the side
of the big dictionary

spread like waterbugs
on the open page:

my hands are close
to being words

Armpit

the Nose runs a ritzy
tobacco shop where
(the moment you enter)

you get the idea
that your shadow
is a plume of smoke

Uvula

the always poising   .
little bunch
of grapes

in anybody's
orgy

Taste Buds

cashews, honey, buttermilk, and lamb
are soils for growing
as many varieties
of wildflower
sandwiches

Spoor

why do I keep stopping
to assign a title

like
        Hangnail
or
        Spit
or
        Peg Leg,

the point is
this: to keep

the juice
going between my

saying it and
your doing it,

you tracking
me and me you

Yawn

(   )

Tic

talk to me
talk to me

Nostrils

get the drift of things
and shape it like a key

Blush

that time
private as blood
comes to light
on my face

like a pocket
pulled inside out

Halfgainer, Halftwist

let your moves

release your love

for this moment

Spit 'n Image

pouring honey:
Benjamin

your face folds
out of mine

& mine is a fold
in grandaddy's sweetness
& so on

faces pour
& fold like honey

Quick

break the seal

on my touch

Groin

the place in the inlet
where two colors
run together, the pure black
creek & the ocean

Hands

the rapids:

domes that bulge
against the current
and troughs
that sluice the whole river

Rice

inside you

my child's hand turning
in grain

in the seed
thrown over us

Caul

what is coming
twill be wrapt

in a burglar's
face for a while

until it's mine
with a new cheek

that feels just
like your leg

Skin

hide nor hair
fish nor feathers

neither beast
nor burden

half one
half another

getting my breath
flat on the ground

Shadow

cold air
between my body

and the figure
flowing down the steps

Trunk

in a sunny room
the dead man's chest
is found to be filled
with wet roots
& chunks of dirt
with the grass still living
& two small grey eggs

Bosoms

apples of the eye
with a tip of a tongue
in each

Balls

another double play

Sweat

a long grip
becomes grease

ice in a sack
turns to money

the old car cranks
like a sweetheart

Birthmark

a wine stain, coffee
bourbon, who knows

what to make of it

II. Choosing

Choosing

for Kittsu

Floating with your head back
up to the ears in a river
you can hear a lot of lives
you didn't expect: an outboard motor
starting up beyond your sight
somebody's sinker taps against a drum
two kids are yelling mouthfuls

In the general flow
are sounds you might make yourself
and ones you can only imagine:
garfish moving along the bottom
water moccasins curling into tree roots
Chickamauga Dam upstream
imperceptibly giving way

Half in air   half in water
your eyes awake   your ears adream
with soundings   the mind can bob
and understand where it is

Alone on the shining surface
buoyed up with creatures
in such a dangerous sleep
I have created children taking chances
underwater   at night
edging with their fingers along the bluff
above the river   jumping barefooted
into a cellar full of broken glass

41

And one recurring child too young to know
what's risky on a ledge
curious only about me down here
too far away to reach him where he turns
like a dummy falling lands flat on his back
each night on the mattress pile of my choice

Safer in my dreams than in his
and falling more certain of love
than the tiny fishlike fact he was
when both of us forgot he might exist
a strange bit of marine life sticking
there on its own bringing up questions
of freewill and time and the possibilities
that we broke
against the motel mirror
in plain water glasses thrown to curse
and celebrate our combining image

Wide awake you chose I chose crash
following crash not him not then but
to lie there accepting floating as we used to
in riverwater filled with silt and muskrats
and sunken boats and boys swimming

For nothing comes of choosing really
in this bed we have fallen into

Lay back your head and listen
to whatever will be with us
to the waters pressing on each eardrum
for the life inside

Goat & Boy

rocking motion of remembering: red pig-iron gate latch

now my feet are on the tree roots   just inside the fence

hyaah   hyaaah   to scare him away   like I've seen done

this goat with eyes broken red inside   his head even

with mine   the horns glance off my shoulder into ivy

the screen door that I run to   is locked from inside

a hoof on the step behind me   then his goatface dressed

in a strand of ivy   waiting for me to take hold of

years ridged into horn   conch shell in my hands

slowly rocking side to side   neither of us with arms

deadlocked in a zodiac of child & goat   a period piece

without a sound or a cry   but moving on its own

Five Ways Down Stringer's Ridge

The evergreen seasonal ridge of the past
                                has no real name.
          Stringer's

                    is two hills over
          and famous

                    but this other
                              with so many sides and differences
          is not
                    so we used the wrong name.

One way down was the west
                    but I should never have tried that.
                                        They were scared

               when I slipped toward the edge
                              on the loose stones
                                        and they should have been.

                         pine cliffs
               and railroad track at the bottom
                         and a long view across half

               the Tennessee and Martin's Island and the other half
                    waist high into Elder Mountain

          They were too young for that look
anyhow
                    so I started back another way.

cut into the west end
is a cove gulley full of vines

    one bankside's shining mudface
           free of leaves
waits for the backswing
  if you didn't jump
     at the very last thinking

      something

I was that pendulum of earth-time
      climbing up the ridge
   into the late air

high above the corn rows and the diesel going home

     on the steep west bluff
  earth-knowing for a year
     before I set out leading children myself thirteen

single file
    up the easy middle path
       that was lined off for a horse trail
      with little logs
        and cleaned-up branches

     the east is a holy room
       owls standing on the wet limbs
     with no leaves anywhere
         just a thin roof
       of pine boughs
     and trailing vines on the floor:

45

black trunks stand around like elders
and keep you from scaring the owls

The memory tries to wander there
          disparate and out of phase
                           makes

     a foot fall   in the odd light.

    The fourth way
        slips between

               the Christmas trees
           along red washed out places
                  on the south side
              where briars grow
          that no one can run through
                no matter how scared

and a last way down
               off behind
       some locked greenhouses
          I can never sneak into now:

       too old to be curious
     about how it is to go
   a different way,
but here I am
       still trying not to find a way down
    Stringer's Ridge
      with all my children though they begin to whine

      trying someway to take all the paths
   and then not be down

to love in all directions
and show the secret places to five more
bands of children:
the bus horns and the cars are signaling
like hawks and crows:
we can hear them through the leaves

warning us

to pick one way
and be down
off Stringer's Ridge.

Link hands little no-names
with your scruffy leader.

This hill is a vague green trance
that I prolong.

Walk out and away
from the ivy house.
Mark the place of no return

here,

say we are late but not ashamed.

Bunched together down there
like a posse
you can tell they are worried

but now they see us
walking out
through the ivy
we are all crying
why are we crying

47

                    afraid we wouldn't get down   afraid
                                we won't go back

hurt

        that we seem to be lost.

Begat Begat

begat begat

stretching back
to Noah's ark and all the coupling
of the lucky few picked to survive
for no reason
the chance pairings   the children
a comedy of muscles
and grace
floating in the memory:
two people changing places
in a red canoe
umbrellas on the water
upside down   full of strawberries

and you are the impulse
warm as an animal saved

and you are the old man
with a trained bird on his shoulder
in a ship that stains the water
with its circus

Feather River Valley, 1956

moving with her
above the stream sound
held by the 4 × 4 stilts
underneath the dance floor
at the back of the restaurant bar
stuck out over the water
I was learning
I am learning

what she has to do with laughing

(that old sound
forming under the floor)

on the kitchen stool
my wife is
another culvertful
of laughing waters
(Minnehaha)
the same substance
the same rushing away

of a dark watery time:

so in the slippery bank sound
all the people-ducks begin

The Literal Snake

A snake was dancing in the waterfall.
I don't know what kind.
We were about halfway up Middle Creek
as it comes down Signal Mountain
our first summer out of college
jumping from big rock
to little precarious rock
when we saw this snake dancing
like a Hindu's rope
in a little off-hand waterfall.
Nevermind what allusions
occur to me now.
All of them occurred to us then
that summer of many animals
and all of them put to rout
with our thumping:
the motorboat left running by itself
in a circle   mumbling at the two of us
coupled in the water
on a submerged stump
at three in the afternoon
with aunts and uncles
coming in the front door back too early
calling Is Anybody Home
while we slip into the Chevrolet
naked as rabbits and always getting away
but never really to ourselves
unless it was laughing at that literal snake
dancing in his waterfall.

The Afterlife

To make a yard
and then think about it
I filled in
between the retaining wall
and the steps
saving what little
dirt for last

The old sofa
went first   then
boxes of psychology
textbooks   a drop-leaf
table with two legs off
(which reminds me)
a pile of mulching
dead limbs and cuttings
flowers   a checkerboard
sacks of garbage periodically

It was a great gradual stew
of artifacts and organisms
(Fold in one half truck sand
garnish lightly with topsoil
and let sit overwinter in rain
Serves two generations)

There was a bony radiator
we threw in
for sacrificial goat
and a refrigerator
hands tied behind him
stood on the edge

oblivious   frozen with dignity
I inspected him for valuables
shut the door gently
like buttoning the top button
on a monument
and pushed him over backwards
on the passionate heap
like my best friend

The yard held its breath
shut in that icebox
for five years
before a boysize graveplot
sunk in freshly on it

Someone might have seen it happen
watery hands picking at the hinges
then after so long
as for a birthday   the breath
released   a soul spreads
into the ground   saying

take it easy   take it easy

The afterlife is not
such a problem

Deposit your old bones
and wornout appliances
so they won't explode
in a cave-in that
might horrify someone
who doesn't know he's
already under the grass
all flesh is

Getting fat and tired and thirty
don't despair at being
something older   something else
What you are is lovely
Andrew Wyeth decay
a shed full of implements
beginning to become land again
part of somebody's yard

The field numbing with yesterday's rain
bloating with liquor and drying out
for the thousandth time
and you   in the midst of it
sighing once for your age
are the slow seeping back and forth
of man into earth
of earth into air

The Truckdriver

a man surprising himself
with care for somebody
who is
out of sight if there at all

what is it
(some mother's charm
against the highway)
makes him take time

> in this dark
> the sun is four broken lines
> on the pavement
> like electric fencing
>
> tuck in your feet
> there's nothing showing
> of two children
> in a big cardboard box
> standing in the righthand lane
> of NC 64 going north
> outside of Hendersonville
>
> when a carwind goes by
> hold it down from inside
>
> this is our house
> to be safe in
> and afraid together

before the truckdriver
will skid to the near shoulder
slam his door and uncover us
like a news item

he will be a father

closed up in a cab
full of too much light
who thinks in the second
instant of seeing it ahead:

my anger   my horsepower
would barrel through
dogs & cows   piles of brush
& rows of boxes
anytime but now

on this morning:

a searching sound like a crownfire
of love and sheer luck (wind and dry branch)
runs with my ignition

The Oracle

Do not ask of me
I am the hooded one

We are here to consult the entrails
for your departure.
About my cave are several signs of life
on the verge of their future
which may be read collectively or not
according to your mood.
Notice that I have no scroll or prepared text
as we approach the first enigma.

This squashed pigeon says one thing,

You are still young

And this black mule, still bubbling,

Do not submit yourself
to your own mind

Upon the cistern ledge this fish
inside a fish inside a fish records that

Life is passed
in the simplest of circles
not in the expanding universe
where everyone's mythologies overlap

And the wormy goat stomach,
what do you think it means? Look closer.
What do you think?
It is a simple admission that

   All advice is vague
   and plagiarized

Ah look, they fly, they fly away,
my beautiful birds, my gulls . . .
an omen of another sort which means,

   A number of changes will come
   and leave you depressed

The fire there which, as you see, is going out
will go out, and this garbage will begin to rot
tomorrow, which all means something else again,

   We shall be left with fragments
   of an order that is not our own

And as you pack these secrets up
and leave me here among my vitals
with a lot of emptied animals,
I must insist that you mean well.

Rock Paintings of the Chumash

Waiting in this hollow air
is what they left:

odd   deserted prints
flushed out in all colors

sumac red   sunburnt ochre
and even blue

spreading shapes
crushed into their own ghost
and floating now on the walls
of caves in Ventura County

like hands beyond pain   cartoons
pointing to a lost civilization:
down there   over here
up beyond the edge: the indications
lead everywhere and I accept them.

From the roof of my mouth
they swim into the bloodstream

mantis   eel   falling clown

virus   cancer   foreign bodies

the comic demigods of disease

that let me imagine fever
is such an art   the playing

of beautiful forming things:
children squashing
through a culvert   laughing
at the bottoms of their shoes
the Chumash   cutting up
on a religious holiday
mixing the paint: one dips

his hand for a brush
with thumb and palm
he makes a red circle   a half-circle
then pushes out the edges
clowning around (with my blood)
making arms and rubbery legs
and fingers that are still
sticky with being alive.

Nickajack Cave

Your recollection burns in my lantern,
shadows me down this ancient tufted ear.
My eyes relax in darkness for your sight.

My hands touch stone that wears water
and I am almost out of sight now almost
gone, but listen for me. I mean to be lost

for years surviving to come out somewhere
telling a tomfool story to filling stations
and chenille shops that will have heard it

before: beneath this place your version,
you long drink of water, is yodeling
like a bloodstream, garbled sleeping sound.

* * *

You are here beside me wondering
if I know where I'm going. You are
there inside singing to a swarming

room. You are the survivor who
found another way out. The cave
itself is nothing but your skull.

You take me past the ribs and kelson
of a pleasure boat through the broken
teeth of an admission stile to where

the audiences don't remember you
with bear hugs for a stranger—to
blank holes filled with history:

the Nickajack tribe and the Union troops
and myself fallen shattered from the ceiling.
You stand with me like sleeping rubble

dreaming of form and you nap in these
cubbyholes hanging upside down
folded in a brotherhood of yourself.

                    * * *

This cave confuses us. Meld of rock
and dung and water. Our voices blend
in a noise that tumbles the lock

of the hill and lets us out—in a chord
that starts the sacred harp again
humming in the earth like a dynamo:

What wondrous love is this
O my soul   O my soul

III. The Swim

The Finger of Necessity

Postal Area #29, Los Angeles

Twice recently young girls have
              given me the finger. The
          first was on the freeway, she

sitting close to her boyfriend turned
              with sure purpose and aimed
          at prominence, seat-belted in

two lanes over. The chemical shock to
              my system made me feel so
          like they wanted I chased them

for miles trying to think of something
              to yell back. The second a few
          minutes ago standing beside a

drugstore would have been easy to
              go back by but I just waved
          like oh another one. It must

be something in the atmosphere, Scorpio
              on the ascendant, or maybe they
          were bored with the just looking

and better this than what I didn't give,
              much better. With one buzzoff
          finger she became the mother

of my invention with her red
        shirt and her hip-huggers
    and her flowered vinyl belt:

Hey cat lady, you eat it.

The Buzzard

the buzzard begins
to feel another buzzard coming on
just once a year   about Eastertime

as though
his brethren had decided on that doctrine
at a huge Baptist convention
somewhere
a long time ago
so he needn't bother himself
about it
flap
and coast   and coast down some
and fly
I've never seen one land
and there are no pictures
of his mating

without publicity   he continues
certain and fundamental in the landscape
neither prosperous nor dwindling
and on a trip you look up
expecting to see him or his child
out one of the car windows
sliding sideways
from your point of view

The Mule

get up under a mule
sometime and look   you

may have heard wrong:
the equipment's all there

dormant   dreaming
of some great mythical

union between species
like Leda & her Swan

or the God-Bull & Europa:
the mule is an aristocrat, one

of the last Classical allusions
in this illiterate world

The African Night Adder

more sensual than any
theologian's dream: the
double penis ornamented
with fringe spikes and sexy
designs like a Deluxe
from the Devil's condom
machine   all ripple
and blind wiggling lust
he can keep one going
and one resting for a full
twenty-four hours and she
can hatch his children
for two years afterward:
Man makes his myths and
the snakes believe them

The Penguin

penguins swim
to migrate
is it spring in the Antarctic
(it's fall here)
are they swimming now
out in the open sea:

listen to them flopping
around our boat   circling
putting us to sleep
looking up at stars
different stars   sweet heart,

a way of loving you
I'd almost forgotten:
penguins rest on their backs
when they're migrating

a star slides
like a piece of ice
down the length of my spine:

part of me is always waiting
for someone to sneak up with love
like that   in the middle
of a poem: a cool two fingers
on my neck   not saying
anything   and part of me
is not waiting for anybody

70

The Dodo, The Griffin

we are all there somewhere
outside   with the animals
and the stars: a band
starting up   a man
connecting constellations
with a dotted line   who says
that darkness is a pouch

the night sky fills
with living things:

        The Flying Kangaroo

        The Burrowing Giraffe

we are never finished
as we are

your words curl up
in my ear like a young girl
reading in her pajamas
about

        The Gryllus

                a legendary
combination of animals: face
of Sophocles, rump of goat,
comb of parrot, bird legs,
fish scales on his back

and he could change into
other combinations
according to the rate
of his pulse   so that when
gryllus mates with gryllus
there is constant metamorphosis

inside such a chaos
conception is a cell
spinning like an old Greek coin:

this moment is beginning

The Flag Page

In the big dictionary
my hand always feels
how slick and neat
the page of imperial
flags, the old ones
little ensign flags
within flags for crown
colonies, moons & stars
& dhows for the Near East
flamboyant clusters
of drums & guidons
for the smallest islands
Tobago   Caledonia
the strong indigenous beasts
of Siam   Malaya
against a white field
or green   such treasure
for some boy's collection
each to be cut out and labeled
in the ledger he tucks away
with gusty secret plans.
But I was looking up a word.

cark

The Moores left us their dog
to take care of, our namesake
Barks   but on a whim
I started calling him Carks.
Such a terror he is
scattering warfare at the poor

73

hedge rabbits like a phantom squad
that never needs to reload
and catching nothing but ticks.
The porch ashtray is full
of the seared little drunkards.
No one gets any good sleep
or work done with that
hangdog underdog around.
What to do with Barks
look at this

^{1}cark /kark/vb (ME carken, lit., to load, burden,
fr. ONF carquier, fr. LL carricare) vt: WORRY
vi: to be anxious
^{2}cark n: TROUBLE, DISTRESS

But that didn't take care of Barks.
He was still there
in spite of how I could fancy his name up
and pencil it to the flag page.
When the sun began to go down
nothing could lure him into arm range
or even rock range.
So one day in the middle of the day
when he was tired
and sacked out in his bones
from a nightful of alarms,
I loaded him in the backseat
and took him to the SPCA.
I'd like to give you a dog.
          What's the matter?
He barks all night.
          It will cost you $5.
It's worth it.

                  What's his name?
Barks.
                  Fits.
Yes. Thank you very much.
                  Not at all.
                  Come back to see us,
                  Mr.
But I was out the door
before he could learn
my crazy name.

The Coyote Cage at the Athens (Ga.) Zoo

You try to sleep but your
damned eyes keep opening
for the dangers of a Sunday

crowd. Last night, every
night, your cage is closest
to where the lovers flip

off and on their convertible
eyes. Nobody could live
like you do, you dumb

beast. Come out of there
and lie down in the grass
with me. Easy. Good boy.

Venus Flytrap

The dumb plant's mouth
closes thoughtfully on a pinch
of ground beef

and my cheap trick
on the green world

backfires: She opens up
early out of phase shows me
a blackened tongue and dies
consciously disappointed.

Hamburger won't do
she could decide
in some brainless, spineless
way within that one
electrical bud.

This was in graduate school
(when I roomed for a while
with a guy in Biochemistry)
and I thought I was learning
something about the decisionmaking
process and digestion
about desire and disillusionment.

When really all it was
was feeling that impulse
die out in her mouth.

Taking a Nap Underneath My Desk

Headfirst in the kneehole
stretched out with my back
on the cool linoleum floor:

The underside of my swivel
chair is a printing press.
This bulletin is just out:

NOTICE
To Duplicate this Desk or if
any Repairs or Keys are or-
dered state Information Below.

JASPER OFFICE FURNITURE CO.
Jasper, Indiana

Desk (Table) No. . . . .
Finish . . . .
Cabinet Maker . . . .
Date Made . . . .
Inspected By . . . .
Finish Sanded By . . . .
Rubbed By . . . .
Trimmed By . . . .
Drawer Lock Key No. . . . .
Drawer Pull No. . . . .
Inspected By . . . .

(Fill in the empty graffiti
blanks yourself)

Why two Inspected By's?
That last must be the Inspector-General.

I would like to meet the man
who makes these places for us.

Places not absolutely private
(Someone could look in the window
and see my legs and feet) or

soundproof (There is a sympathetic
humming with the air conditioning) but

suitable for the Professional Nap.
They might be marketed as Indoor

Gazebos (quartersize) or Special
New Supine Confessionals (with

drawers) or Thinking Cells (fully
paneled): a shepherd's hut

Hiking in the Alps at dusk I come upon this shelter
dry and clean   I have been here a week now
deliriously happy   When I decide to leave I will
climb the next ridge and see the towers of a town
I had no idea I was so close to civilization

The desk drawer pushes out
from the back. A beautiful blank
space reveals itself. I ought to
write something there: *Mickey
loves Virginia May 29, 1842—
5th Illinois Cavalry—Croatan*

The mailcoach: Stowed away in the compartment where
freshly cut flowers are shipped   On either side of me
long-stemmed roses and six-foot irises are trying to stay
alive by lying very still   I am a gift for somebody

        who knocks on the office door.
        Two little questioning raps.
        I will never know who it was.
        No footsteps coming or going.
        My big clomping shoes are floating
        three feet above the bookshelf.

Sent to repair the split face of a giant wooden man (St. Jude)
who stares out over Helsinki   He has a clockface
in his forehead   two hundred feet from the ground   I am
clinging dangerously to the inside of one of his coffin-shaped
nostrils   How could they expect me to use hammer and nail
up here when all my strength must be saved for hanging on
It occurs to me that this is the only way to fix a saint's face
the crack in his features slowly healing for the pendulum
of my weight in his sinuses   I am the famous
Helsinki Boogerman   special counsel to the wooden clergy
Hello Up In There, ole silent father,
Hello Behind The Clock

        God of the Cave this afternoon
        I am dormant finally in a ceremony
        sleep is a part of.

Late August

preparing for September
my notes had better not get rained on
I don't remember anything I read
past turning the page
my handwriting is on its own
to say something intelligent
I can't help out any longer
Class,

      cracked wheat bread
      is goodstuff

      on the night porch
      lean back in a heap
      of just-dried clothes
      from the laundromat
      warm as a wife
      gone to bed early
      an hour ago

      the small of her back
      here against the
      small of mine

Waking Up

I am a fresh tongue
resting in this grave

where nothing needs to be said.
The milky lid of a glimpse

covers all. My head is a trick
egg neatly full of my family

and salt. Now you see it
now you don't. So

the act begins.
My walk-on pantomime

beloved of all ages. Watch
as I wash up and shave

and discover (in a wild
surmise) Bacon! Fork!

Keats

beneath whatever kind of shirt
his shoulders are whales again
moving now under gardens in Italy

his face turns like a monastery
in the afternoon

his feet begin to loosen
and make furrows in the soil

his elbows rise
from gravel to perch

the trees fill up their lungs
and wait

when he arrives
we stand up and stretch ourselves
like the fingers of his hand

Witchdoctor

Asleep the faces
of my children come
to the foot of the bed
scared to wake me up
by having to.

> *My dreaming face*
> *is a pine cone in mid-air*
>
> *Just above the lake surface*
> *a double dragonfly*
>
> *witchdoctor*
>
> *Loft one rock in the memory*
> *the far chunking sound*
> *and closer in   skipping twice*
> *becomes this black child's face*
> *is a dark egg I hold*
> *in my hand   I have thrown*

I am awake.

There are children all around
my bed

that I can actually touch.

Easter Morning Ride

In the old Blue Goose
out to the covered bridge
and the waterfall below it
and coming back the sunlights
off the tracks close to the road
made me think (eventually)
Some places slide at just
the speed of our eyes before
they bend and look away.

The Swim

It's so easy to say
I want a new life
in the form of some new shoes
a new dark-blue turtleneck
and a big scruffy poncho
for poetry reading
a whole new set of people
a new wife new town
new children. So have one.

Stretch like the cat in her sleep.

A tissue catches fire
in a child's hand
and floats up burning
out of a basement window.

I am hunched over, standing
inside a waterfall
and I can spot figures out there.
Watery bodies
come clear to one eye
clear and then gone

& I'm just as much of a blur
a nameless hump in the shower
hoping, with this poem,
to go with it down
that slick place
into the drink
of a swim, my shoulders
in the moving body.